# Talking
# IRL

# Talking

## Conversation Starters

## for When You

## HAVE

# IRL:

## to Talk to
## Someone

UNIVERSE

Robb Pearlman

# CONTENTS

# INTRODUCTION

Today's technology offers us more ways to communicate with one another than ever before. Whether it's text, email, apps, or even tweets and DMs, as well as the variety of dating apps, the vast majority of these methods of communication have built a virtual firewall between people that keeps them from ever engaging in actual face-to-face contact.

Emails, especially those concerning business or other more serious matters, afford us the opportunity to get straight to the point. The subject line of the email clearly states what the purpose or topic the body of the email is concerned with, and the content is straightforward. Texts, which usually cover more personal or informal topics, are by design intended to be short, with abbreviations, acronyms, and emojis used in place of spelled-out words, phrases, or sentences. The good news is that in each of these methods, even if conducted in real time, these technologies have made conversations more efficient and productive. Ironically, even though communication seems faster, we still have to take the time to type everything into our phones or computers, and we're given more time to think about what we're going to say so we can carefully consider what we're saying, how we're saying it, and what the potential reaction to what we're saying will be.

But sometimes, despite your best efforts, as much as you won't want to, you're going to have to talk to another person.

I know, I know. It's *the worst*.

But not all emails get through. Some details cannot be properly communicated via emoji. And sometimes, if you're not careful, your phone is going to run out of power and you'll look up to see yourself surrounded by other people IRL.

And when you find yourself in a situation in which you have to talk to another person, it's going to be really weird, and probably unintelligible, if you talk the way you text. You're going to have to, at least to some degree, surround the main topic with niceties. That's called small talk. And chances are you have no idea how to do it.

This book will help you figure out what to say, and what not to say, after "Hello."

# OUT AND ABOUT

Technology has afforded us the opportunity to do most everything from the comfort of our homes. You can shop for pretty much anything and have it delivered to your door. Books, clothing, furniture, groceries, and toys can all show up, boxed and even gift wrapped, on our welcome mats. Nightly meals can arrive packed and iced. You can meet an LTR or DTF with a swipe. You can even buy a car online. But, every once in a while, you will be forced to leave your home. And when you do, you may also have to engage in small talk.

# Contents

# 1

# GROCERY SHOPPING

When browsing through merchandise, you may encounter a shopper. Do not panic. This is a shopper's natural habitat and, as long as they're not provoked by your snatching that bag of frozen peas they were reaching for, interactions should be relatively calm.

# Talking IRL IDEAS

IF THE PERSON IS HOLDING A GROCERY ITEM
YOU HAVE INTEREST IN, ASK:

- WHAT DO YOU THINK ABOUT [THE PRODUCT]?
- HOW DO YOU PREPARE/USE IT?
- HOW DOES IT COMPARE TO OTHER BRANDS
  OR VARIETIES?
> NOW TALK ABOUT HOW YOU HEARD ABOUT THE
  PRODUCT, WHAT YOU PLAN TO DO WITH IT, OR
  WHAT YOU KNOW ABOUT ITS OTHER USES.

# MORE Talking IRL IDEAS

IF YOU'RE IN THE PRODUCE AISLE, ASK HOW THEY CAN TELL IF A FRUIT OR VEGETABLE IS RIPE.

TRY FOLLOWING UP WITH:

> DESCRIBE YOUR METHOD AND/OR AN OUTLANDISH METHOD YOU'VE HEARD OF.

## BTW

*As wonderfully convenient as online shopping may be, it's also important to support your local independent retailers. You may pay a little more—and have to pay a little more attention—but it's worth it when you remember (and remind others) that we are all part of a society that relies on one another for meaningful social interaction. To a point.*

> > > > > > > > > > > > > > > > > > > > > > > > > > > > > > > > > > > >

# FYI

## > BLACK FRIDAY <

*Unless you're lined up outside a store for sixteen hours and have to get to know the people waiting with you so you can share the costs of the pizzas you're ordering to keep fortified until the lights turn on, there's no time—or need to talk—during a Black Friday sale.*

*Just shut up, fully embrace the nihilistic materialism that generations of corporate marketing have infused straight into your marrow and run like Forrest Gump ran to Jenny over to that discounted merchandise. If someone wishes to saunter around the harshly lit aisles while thumbing through the holiday flyer and chatting with passersby, that's their problem.*

# IN A COFFEE SHOP

Coffee shops are the modern-day town squares. Would-be playwrights, wannabe novelists, and social-media influencers of all stripes gather among knitting circles, students, retirees, and work-from-homers to plug their ears with headphones, keep their heads down, and drink dangerous amounts of caffeine.

# Talking IRL IDEAS

IF YOU FIND YOURSELF ON A LONG OR
SLOW-MOVING LINE, ASK THE PERSON IN
FRONT OF OR BEHIND YOU:

• HOW LONG HAVE YOU BEEN WAITING?

> NOW COMMENT ABOUT THE USUAL SPEED
(OR LACK THEREOF) IN THE ESTABLISHMENT.

## BTW

*If the chat takes on a decidedly negative or complaining tone, be sure to keep your voice low so it's drowned out by the noise made by the frother; otherwise, the counterperson may hear you and add something more than a shot of vanilla to your latte.*

> > > > > > > > > > > > > > > > > > > > > > > > > > > > > > >

# MORE Talking IRL IDEAS

## IF THE WAIT TIME ON LINE DRAGS EVEN LONGER, ASK:

- HOW OFTEN DO YOU COME TO THE SHOP?
- ARE YOU A FREQUENT PATRON?

## BTW

*If you recognize the person on line with you, it's okay to mention seeing them before, but be sure to do it in a light or breezy tone so as to not sound like a creep. There's a difference between "I've seen you here before" and "I've. Seen. You. Here. Before."*

## WHILE ORDERING, ASK THE BARISTA:

- HOW IS YOUR DAY GOING?
- IS IT SLOWER OR BUSIER THAN USUAL?
- > AGREE WITH THE BARISTA'S REASONING FOR THE INFLUX OR LACK OF CUSTOMERS.
- > DISAGREEING WITH THEIR ASSESSMENT WILL MAKE IT SEEM AS IF YOU'RE EXPLAINING THEIR OWN BUSINESS TO THEM. THIS IS A BAD IDEA, AS YOU WILL SOUND LIKE A KNOW-IT-ALL MAN- OR WOMANSPLAINER WHO DESERVES TO GET REGULAR INSTEAD OF DECAF.

# FYI

## > TALL IS SMALL <

Unless you have romantic motives, do not ask when their shift ends or when they get a break. Simply comment that they work so hard you hope they get a break or can leave at a reasonable time.

>>>>>>>>>>>>>>>>>>>>>>>>>>>>>>>>>>>>>>>>>>>

Though most coffee-shop patrons want to keep to themselves and focus their attention on their work or entertainment, there are going to be people hanging out for the sole purpose of passing the time in enjoying a cup of joe and engaging others in pleasant conversation. Depending on the seating configurations of the establishment, and whether or not the piped-in music is loud enough to drown out conversation, you may find yourself engaged with someone who'd like to chat.

If you see someone sitting with only a beverage, wide-eyed, and the palpable energy of someone looking to talk, you may want to find somewhere else to sit.

## MORE Talking IRL IDEAS

BUT IF THERE'S NOWHERE ELSE TO SIT,
AND THEY INTRODUCE THEMSELVES, ASK:
• HOW IS YOUR DAY GOING?

> > > > > > > > > > > > > > > > > > > > > > > > > > > > > > > > > > > > > >

NOTE THAT THIS QUESTION IS LIKE "HOW ARE YOU?" (SEE PAGE 29). IT IS A POLITE QUESTION, BUT BE PREPARED TO HEAR EXACTLY HOW THEIR DAY IS GOING.

> IF IT'S GOING WELL, SAY HOW GLAD YOU ARE FOR THEM.

> IF IT'S NOT GOING WELL, BE PREPARED TO OFFER WORDS OF ENCOURAGEMENT OR INSPIRATION TO GET THEM PAST THEIR DIFFICULTY.

## BTW

*If the conversation turns particularly dark or troublesome, do not run screaming away. Instead offer to fire up your laptop and search for certified therapists or other professionals to help them through their troubles.*

# MORE Talking IRL IDEAS

IF THE PERSON IS READING A BOOK OR MAGAZINE
OR WATCHING A MOVIE OR TV SHOW, ASK:

• DO YOU LIKE THE BOOK/ARTICLE/MOVIE/SHOW?

• HAVE YOU READ/SEEN OTHER THINGS ON THE
SAME TOPIC?

• WOULD YOU RECOMMEND IT?

> TRY FOLLOWING UP WITH YOUR FAVORITE OR
SOMETHING SIMILAR TO RECOMMEND.

> > > > > > > > > > > > > > > > > > > > > > > > > > > > > > > > > > > >

If you or they are working on a computer, chances are they will engage you first with a seemingly innocuous question: They will ask what you're working on. Be as brief and vague as possible because there's a good chance the person has started conversation for the sole purpose of seizing on the opportunity to let you know what they're working on. Try not to take the bait. If you ask what they're writing, they will tell you, in excruciating detail, about the mythological world they've created that will span ten books and twelve feature films.

## BUT IF IT'S UNAVOIDABLE, ASK:

- WHAT INSPIRED YOU TO WRITE?
- WHY, IN PARTICULAR, THIS PROJECT?
> TALK ABOUT YOUR ARTISTIC ENDEAVORS.

# BTW

YOU MAY BE FORCED IN A POSITION, ESPECIALLY AFTER YOUR THIRD CUP OF COFFEE, TO ASK SOMEONE TO WATCH YOUR BELONGINGS WHILE YOU USE THE RESTROOM.

> ONCE YOU'VE RETURNED, THANK THEM FOR WATCHING YOUR THINGS AND OFFER TO DO THE SAME FOR THEM.

> RELAY A BRIEF ANECDOTE ABOUT A TIME YOUR THINGS WENT MISSING.

>>>>>>>>>>>>>>>>>>>>>>>>>>>>>>>>>>>>>>>>>

# FYI

## > 'SUP? <

*Many retail and service industry professionals are paid to make small talk with you in order to get a commission, make a sale, or simply provide good customer service. Be polite and friendly, but there's no need to stress about what to say to them or how to respond to their queries. Even if you're asked, you are under no obligation to explain why your name is spelled as it is to the barista.*

# 3
# ON A TRIP

Let's be honest: modern train or air travel is, at best, uncomfortable and, at worst, torturous. Long lines, small seats, delays, and exorbitant prices have forced people into treating the act of traveling as more of a tactical military exercise than the start or end of a grand adventure.

If you find yourself in a travel situation where everything goes smoothly, then take a moment to reward yourself or thank your higher power, because either the universe is thanking you for a past kindness or miracles do, indeed, happen.

Chances are, though, you're going to find yourself in a situation in which you have to talk to your fellow travelers.

# Talking IRL IDEAS

IF YOU'RE SITTING NEXT TO SOMEONE WHO
CLEARLY WANTS TO TALK RATHER THAN SIT
QUIETLY AND LET THE JET ENGINES DROWN OUT
CONVERSATION, ASK:

• WHERE ARE YOU FROM? WHERE ARE YOU GOING?

> NOW YOU SAY WHERE YOU'RE FROM AND WHERE
  YOU'RE GOING.

> ASK FOR RECOMMENDATIONS FOR RESTAURANTS
  OR PLACES TO VISIT.

TRY FOLLOWING UP WITH:

• ARE YOU TRAVELING FOR PLEASURE OR BUSINESS?

> NOW GIVE YOUR REASONS.

> TALK ABOUT HOW OFTEN YOU'VE MADE THIS TRIP.

# 4

# WALKING A DOG

Do not make small talk with dogs you pass on the street. Instead:

After getting permission from their owner, introduce yourself by letting the dog sniff the back of your hand, say "Hello [dog's name], my name is [your name]," and proceed to tell the good boy or girl how perfect they are (there is a 100 percent chance that they will be perfect) as well as your deepest secrets, fondest wishes, and everyday fears. You will have no trouble talking for as long as time and the owner allow.

But before you can talk to a dog, you will, unfortunately, have to make small talk with their owner first. Keep all small talk as dog-centric as possible. (You both know the owner is a means to an end.) No need to introduce yourself, as the only name that matters is the dog's.

# Talking IRL IDEAS

## SAY TO THE OWNER:

- HOW CUTE/BIG/FUZZY/PERFECT YOUR DOG IS!
- WHAT IS YOUR NAME? (THE NAME OF THE DOG, NOT THE OWNER—THE OWNER'S NAME IS COMPLETELY UNIMPORTANT.)
- MAY I INTRODUCE MYSELF TO YOUR PUP?

## BTW

*Once you're done sharing quality time with your new friend, thank the owner (but not by name as it's so unimportant you don't remember if you ever knew it) for introducing you to [dog's name] (a name you not only remember but will want to tattoo on your arm as a constant reminder), and say good-bye. To the dog.*

# 5
# ON AN ELEVATOR

Don't *ever* make small talk on an elevator.

Don't.

Just get on, push the button for your floor, stare straight ahead or at your phone while waiting, and exit when the doors open.

The only thing you should ever say on an elevator is, "What floor may I push for you?" if you're standing near the buttons, or, "Excuse me, please," if you're standing in the back and need to get past people to exit.

# FYI

## > THANK YOU, NEXT. <

*When, as a greeting, someone says, "Hi, how are you?" what that really means is "Hi." They don't really want to know how you are. Even if you think they really do, they don't. It's just something to say that indicates they're willing, to some degree, to engage in small talk with you. So unless the query is coming from a health professional while you're lying in a hospital bed, just reply with, "Hi. Good, thanks. How are you?"*

# 6

# NEVER-EVERS

There are some topics (e.g., personal or sensitive) that are better suited for times when you're really trying to get to know someone, like on a date, or after you've known a person long enough to build a mutual sense of trust and friendship.

## UNTIL THAT TIME, IT'S OKAY TO ASK ABOUT SOMEONE'S FAMILY, BUT NEVER, EVER ASK:

> IF THEY ARE PREGNANT

> WHY THEY ARE NOT MARRIED

> WHY THEY DO NOT HAVE CHILDREN

IT'S OKAY TO ASK SOMEONE'S OCCUPATION, BUT NEVER, EVER ASK:

> HOW MUCH MONEY THEY EARN

IF YOU ARE IN A GYM OR OTHER FITNESS/ ATHLETIC SETTING, IT'S OKAY TO ASK ABOUT SOMEONE'S FITNESS ROUTINE, SPORT OR ACTIVITY OF CHOICE, OR DIET, BUT NEVER, EVER ASK:

> HOW OLD THEY ARE
> HOW MUCH THEY WEIGH
> WHY THEY LOOK/DRESS/ACT THE WAY THEY DO
> WHAT IS "WRONG" WITH THEM

# EVENTS

When life hands you lemons, make lemonade. And if you have to attend a party or social event, try limes as they go better in margaritas.

For better or worse, there will be times when—because of familial obligation, social standing, or your own doing—you're going to have to be in a group of people. And talk to them.

Hopefully you'll be surrounded by people you know, but social circles are getting wider every day, so you may be faced with talking to friends of friends, partners of relatives, or even partners of your relative's friends. And though a bad DJ or cash bar might dampen your spirits, talking to strangers or acquaintances shouldn't keep you from having a good time.

# Contents

# AT A BIRTHDAY PARTY

The only thing worse than attending someone's birthday party, where you're expected to make small talk with the guest of honor and maybe a few other people, is attending your own birthday party, where you're expected to make small talk with *everyone*.

# Talking IRL IDEAS

IF YOU'RE AT SOMEONE ELSE'S PARTY,
ASK ABOUT A PERSON'S RELATIONSHIP TO
THE GUEST OF HONOR:

- HOW DO YOU KNOW THE BIRTHDAY BOY/GIRL?
- > NOW TALK ABOUT **YOUR** RELATIONSHIP WITH THE
  PERSON, LIKE HOW LONG YOU'VE KNOWN THEM,
  AND/OR WHERE YOU MET.

# BTW

*If it involves the phrase "you had to be there," then do
not explain private jokes you share with the Birthday Boy/Girl. The
jokes won't be funny to other people because they had to be there.*

# MORE Talking IRL IDEAS

## SOMEONE ELSE'S BIRTHDAY PARTY CUE #1:
## OH LOOK, THERE'S CAKE.

- WHAT KIND OF CAKE DO YOU LIKE?
- WHAT KIND OF CAKE DO YOU NOT LIKE?

> NOW DESCRIBE YOUR FAVORITE AND MOST HATED DESSERTS, WHERE YOU GET THEM, AND ASK IF THE PERSON HAS EVER TASTED IT/BEEN THERE.

> ENCOURAGE PEOPLE TO TRY YOUR FAVORITE DESSERTS.

## FYI

### > GOTTA GO <

*Do not talk about your intestinal, gut, or colon-related reactions to eating too much cake, dairy, or desserts.*

## SOMEONE ELSE'S BIRTHDAY PARTY CUE #2: GIFTS!

- THE BIRTHDAY BOY/GIRL IS SO HARD TO BUY FOR. THEY SEEM TO HAVE EVERYTHING. WHAT DID YOU GET THEM?

## TRY FOLLOWING UP WITH:

> DESCRIBE YOUR GIFT, AND WHY YOU THOUGHT IT WAS APPROPRIATE.

> TALK ABOUT THE TROUBLE/EASE YOU HAD IN WRAPPING IT.

## BTW

*Do not talk about how you re-gifted your present because you didn't like it.*

# MORE Talking IRL IDEAS

SOMEONE ELSE'S BIRTHDAY PARTY CUE #3:
GREAT, NOW THERE'S THE SINGING OF THE
"HAPPY BIRTHDAY" SONG.

• I USUALLY MOUTH THE WORDS TO THIS SONG.
  HOW ABOUT YOU?

## FYI

### > NOBODY CARES <

Do not talk about the issues regarding copyright and payment to the heirs of the people who wrote the song—nobody cares.

Do talk about when your family, friends, and wait staff embarrassed you by singing "Happy Birthday" to you in a restaurant.

If you're the Birthday Boy/Girl, it's your responsibility
to greet the attendees, which sounds a lot worse
than it probably is, considering the guests are there
because, presumably, you know them all and have some
relationship. You may, however, need to make small talk
with their partners, spouses, or dates.

## AT YOUR OWN BIRTHDAY PARTY, HERE IS THE EASIEST WAY TO BEGIN SMALL TALK:

- THANK YOU SO MUCH FOR COMING TO MY BIRTHDAY PARTY!

## IF THE PERSON BROUGHT A GIFT:

- THANK YOU! I WILL UNWRAP IT LATER.
- > IF THE PERSON **INSISTS** YOU OPEN IT NOW, DO SO AND THANK THEM FOR THEIR GENEROSITY AND KINDNESS.

## IF THE PERSON DID NOT BRING A GIFT:

- > EXPLAIN THAT NO GIFTS WERE NECESSARY, EVEN IF YOU'RE **DISAPPOINTED**.
- > **POLITELY SAY** YOU SEE SOMEONE ELSE WHO JUST ARRIVED AND YOU NEED TO TALK TO HIM/HER, BUT YOU'LL BE RIGHT BACK.
- > **DO NOT** GO RIGHT BACK IF YOU DON'T WANT TO.

# BTW

*There's a difference between a friend and someone being friendly. Being friends with someone means you can sit beside them in a crowded movie theater without the pressure of making small talk. Being friendly with someone means you should say, "Hello" to a stranger when they first sit next to you in a movie theater and then never speak to again. In brief: nobody—and I mean nobody—wants to hear what anyone else has to say during a movie so be a good person and just be quiet.*

> > > > > > > > > > > > > > > > > > > > > > > > > > > > > > > > > >

# MORE Talking IRL IDEAS

## IF YOU'RE THE BIRTHDAY BOY/GIRL, ASK ABOUT TRAVEL:

- DID YOU DRIVE HERE? OR TAKE PUBLIC TRANSPORTATION?
- WHAT ROUTE DID YOU TRAVEL?

## TRY FOLLOWING UP WITH:

- HOW LONG DID IT TAKE?
  OR
- WHERE DID YOU PARK?

# BTW

*Do not suggest alternate routes after the fact.*

# FYI

## > SRSLY <

*If the person has come very far and plans on drinking, offer to let them stay with you so they don't have to get home late.*

# ② AT A WEDDING

Whether or not you're part of the wedding party, if you're single and have been invited without a "plus one" or if you rip your pants doing a death drop on the dance floor, weddings can be fraught with drama. Especially if you have to talk to people you don't know.

## BTW

*If you're attending with a "plus-one," you'll be able to share the small-talk responsibilities by never leaving each other's side, which will force people to engage both of you at the same time.*

*This affords you the opportunity to plan beforehand, so use the weeks and days before the event, or even the car ride to the reception, to think of four or five topics of conversation that you can recycle from one conversation with a stranger to another.*

# Talking IRL IDEAS

IF YOU'RE AT SOMEONE'S WEDDING (AND
YOU'RE NOT RELATED TO THEM), ASK ABOUT
THE PERSON'S RELATIONSHIP TO THE GUEST OF
HONOR:
• HOW DO YOU KNOW THE BRIDE(S) OR GROOM(S)?

IF THE PERSON IS A COWORKER, BUSINESS
ASSOCIATE, OR OTHERWISE PROFESSIONALLY
AFFILIATED, ASK:
• HOW LONG HAVE YOU BEEN WITH THE COMPANY,
  AND WHAT DO YOU DO? (SEE PAGES 60 TO 79 FOR
  MORE BUSINESS-RELATED IDEAS.)

# MORE Talking IRL IDEAS

## IF THE PERSON IS A NEIGHBOR OF THE COUPLE'S, ASK:

- HOW LONG HAVE YOU LIVED THERE?
- DO YOU LIKE THE NEIGHBORHOOD/CITY/TOWN?
- > IF **YOU'VE VISITED** THE NEIGHBORHOOD/CITY/TOWN, TALK ABOUT RESTAURANTS, PARKS, OR OTHER POINTS OF INTEREST THAT YOU LIKE.
- > IF **YOU'VE NEVER BEEN**, OFFER REGRETS FOR NEVER VISITING, AND ASK FOR IDEAS OF WHAT TO DO OR SEE.
- > FOLLOW UP BY TALKING ABOUT **YOUR** NEIGHBORHOOD AND RELATIONSHIPS, IF ANY, WITH YOUR NEIGHBORS.
- > NOW TALK ABOUT **YOUR** RELATIONSHIP WITH THE BRIDE(S) OR GROOM(S), LIKE HOW LONG YOU'VE KNOWN THEM, AND/OR WHERE YOU MET.

# SOMEONE ELSE'S WEDDING CUE #1: THE FOOD. IF THE FOOD IS GOOD, SAY:

- THIS IS SO MUCH BETTER THAN THE USUAL RUBBERY CHICKEN OR DRY FISH AT SOME OTHER RECEPTIONS I'VE BEEN TO.*

# TRY FOLLOWING UP WITH:

- WHAT WAS THE WORST WEDDING FOOD YOU EVER HAD?
- > NOW SAY WHAT WAS YOUR WORST EXPERIENCE.

*This should not be said if the reception you're referencing was hosted by, or in celebration of, the person you're talking to.

# MORE Talking IRL IDEAS

SOMEONE ELSE'S WEDDING CUE #2: THE VENUE.
IF YOU'RE AT A DESTINATION WEDDING, ASK
ABOUT THEIR TRAVEL EXPERIENCE:

- HOW WAS YOUR FLIGHT/DRIVE?
- DO YOU HAVE A PREFERRED AIRLINE/ROUTE?
- WHAT IS YOUR FAVORITE HOTEL / SHORT-TERM
  RENTAL PROPERTY OR SERVICE?
> TRY FOLLOWING UP WITH **YOUR** OWN
  EXPERIENCE(S), AND SAY HOW GLAD YOU ARE TO
  TAKE A VACATION.*

*Say this even if you're not and the whole thing is a terrible expense
and inconvenience, but you felt such an overwhelming sense of
obligation to attend that you maxed out your credit cards and used up
all of your remaining vacation days.

## IF THE WEDDING IS IN YOUR CITY OR TOWN, ASK:

- HOW LONG DID IT TAKE YOU TO GET HERE?
- WHAT ROUTE DID YOU TAKE?
- HAVE YOU ATTENDED AN EVENT AT THIS VENUE BEFORE?

# 3

# AT YOUR OWN WEDDING

There's a pretty good chance that if you're at your own wedding, the person you're marrying will help you shoulder the burden of small talk with distant relatives, plus-ones, and friends of your mother's, who, had they not been invited, would have surely caused any number of social cataclysms.

Better yet, because you and your new spouse are the center of attention (barring drunken members of the wedding party), everyone will understand that you have to mingle with all of the guests and, therefore, need to limit each conversation to just a few minutes.

# Talking IRL IDEAS

RECYCLE EACH CHAT A FEW TIMES (OR A FEW DOZEN OR FEW HUNDRED TIMES) BY STICKING TO A SIMPLE GREETING AND SAYING:

• THANK YOU FOR ATTENDING AND FOR YOUR GIFT.

• HAVE YOU HAD ENOUGH TO EAT OR DRINK?

> AND THEN MOVE ON TO THE **NEXT GUEST.**

## IF YOU'RE CORNERED BY A WEDDING GUEST, WITHOUT YOUR SPOUSE:

- I HAVEN'T SEEN YOU SINCE ____. IT'S BEEN TOO LONG. WHAT HAVE YOU BEEN UP TO?
- > TRY FOLLOWING UP BY ASKING TO HEAR ABOUT (POSITIVE) THINGS SUCH AS NEW JOBS, RELATIONSHIPS, OR VACATIONS.

## IF THEY'RE MARRIED:

- WHAT DO YOU REMEMBER BEST ABOUT YOUR WEDDING DAY?
- > IF YOU WERE AT THEIR WEDDING, AGREE THAT WHATEVER THEY SAID WAS, INDEED, MEMORABLE.
- > IF YOU WERE NOT AT THE WEDDING, AGREE THAT IT SOUNDS AS IF IT WAS GREAT.

# FYI

## > DOUBLE-REVERSE WHITE LIE <

*If they ask what you've been up to, say that all of your time has been spent planning the day's big event then, pretend to see your spouse across the room and confide that your spouse needs you to rescue them from making small talk with someone.*

# 4
# ON A DATE

In most circumstances, small talk is meant to fill time with light conversation before, during, or after any actual reason you and the other person are brought together. But the entire mechanism of dating is based on employing light conversation in order to get know someone: therefore, small talk, as such, is the perilous fulcrum upon which your future as a couple rests.

Tip too much to one side and you'll come off as being aloof and distant. Weighing too much on the other will make you seem as desperate as Gollum going after a ring, engagement or otherwise. And inserting too many unexpected and tangential nerd references may make you seem out of their league (amirite?!).

Nevertheless, statistically speaking, your wedding is not being prearranged by your nineteenth-century Russian milkman father, so you've probably had some conversations, either via app, text, or email, with the person you're on the date with, and some of the basic groundwork has already been laid.

(Also, statistically speaking, you didn't immediately get that *Fiddler on the Roof* reference, which rests in the same pile of desirable talking points as *The Lord of the Rings* one.)

## Talking IRL IDEAS

**WHEN ON A DATE, TRY ASKING:**

• WHERE DID YOU GROW UP?

• WHEN DID YOU MOVE HERE?

> TRY FOLLOWING UP WITH WHERE **YOU'RE** ORIGINALLY FROM AND WHY YOU MOVED TO THE AREA.

• WHAT'S YOUR TYPICAL WEEKEND LIKE?

> NOW SUGGEST SOME OF **YOUR** FAVORITE ACTIVITIES.

# MORE Talking IRL IDEAS

IF YOU MET ONLINE, TALK ABOUT YOUR USE OF THE DATING SITE OR APP: FOCUS NOT ON THE NUMBERS OR SUCCESSES, BUT ON THE FUNNY, STRANGE, AND OTHERWISE G-RATED MISHAPS THAT MAKE FOR LIGHTHEARTED STORIES OF DATING LIFE:

• WHAT'S YOUR FUNNIEST DATE STORY?

# BTW

*In any small-talk conversation (but especially during a date), you really need to listen to what the other person is saying so you can respond and determine, with substantial if not reasonable certainty, whether or not this is someone you want to be in a relationship with (long-term or otherwise).*

# FYI

## > TMI <

*If the conversation turns to having children, marriage goals, out-of-country career paths, or other topics that clearly state your or your date's long-term plans, plan for the date—if not the relationship—to end immediately.*

5

# RELIGION **AND** POLITICS

There are topics you should avoid bringing up when first meeting someone.

As a general rule, abstain from talking about anything that would start an argument, including and especially religion and politics. The only time it's okay to have small talk about religion with a complete stranger is if—and only if—you are in a temple, mosque, church, or other house of worship and you both agree on the inalienable rights afforded to all faiths by the United States Constitution.

The only time it's okay to talk about politics is if you're at a rally, fundraiser, or other political event and you both agree that Nazis are bad.

# FYI

## > HOW DOES THIS MAKE YOU FEEL? <

*Small talk should be used to fill up some time or get to know someone a little better. It is not meant to be a platform to work out your personal issues. Save that for your mother or your therapist. Or, if your issues are with your mother, just your therapist.*

# OFFICE WORK

The reason they call work "work" and not "fun" is that no matter how much fun you're having at work, it's still work and not fun—especially in an office.

Unless you work alone or from home with only your dog or cat for company, you spend a lot of time with coworkers with whom you're going to have to converse, particularly in a trendy but soul-crushing open-office floorplan filled with cubicles. For many, one of the least fun parts of work is having to figure out what to say to coworkers, clients, or bosses when you're not in a meeting about quarterly reports or forecasts or other things people have fun talking about.

# Contents

1

# IN A MEETING (WITH CLIENTS OR OTHER NON-COLLEAGUES)

Your colleagues are caught in traffic or waiting on line for their Frappuccinos, and you find yourself in a conference room or on a conference call making small talk with a business partner. You're the face of your company (or at least the voice), so your job is to set a positive, productive, and enthusiastic tone for the meeting.

Stick to topics that feel neither too personal nor have the potential to veer into negativity or complaints. Steer the conversation to either work-related topics or those tangentially related to work.

# Talking IRL IDEAS

**WHILE YOU'RE WAITING FOR YOUR COLLEAGUES, ASK:**

- HOW LONG HAVE YOU BEEN WITH YOUR COMPANY?
- > NOW DESCRIBE HOW LONG **YOU'VE** BEEN AT **YOUR** COMPANY.
- WHERE IS YOUR COMPANY LOCATED?

**TRY FOLLOWING UP WITH:**

- DO YOU LIKE THE AREA?
- HOW LONG IS YOUR COMMUTE?
- DO YOU DRIVE OR TAKE PUBLIC TRANSPORTATION?
- > NOW DESCRIBE **YOUR** COMMUTE.

# MORE Talking IRL IDEAS

## TO KEEP THE CONVERSATION GOING EVEN LONGER:

- IS THERE A TRADITIONALLY BUSY AND/OR QUIET TIME AT WORK?
- > NOW **AGREE** THAT A REALLY BUSY AND/OR A REALLY QUIET TIME AT WORK IS THE WORST/THE BEST.
- DOES YOUR JOB REQUIRE ANY TRAVEL?

## TRY FOLLOWING UP WITH:

- WHERE HAVE YOU GONE RECENTLY?
- WHERE WILL YOU BE GOING?
- > NOW DESCRIBE **YOUR** RECENT TRAVELS.

# IF ON A CONFERENCE OR VIDEO CALL, ASK:

- WHAT'S THE WEATHER LIKE WHERE YOU ARE?
> NOW DESCRIBE THE WEATHER WHERE **YOU** ARE.
- WHERE ARE YOU CALLING FROM? DO YOU NEED TO USE A CONFERENCE ROOM OR DO YOU HAVE YOUR OWN OFFICE?
> NOW DESCRIBE **YOUR** OFFICE LAYOUT.

# FOLLOW UP BY COMPLAINING ABOUT OPEN FLOORPLANS, AND CUBICLES.

> MENTION THE INEVITABILITY OF PEOPLE **TALKING OVER** ONE ANOTHER DURING THE SESSION.
> **LAMENT** THE RELIANCE ON TECHNOLOGY, BUT **ADMIT** IT'S CHEAPER AND MORE EFFICIENT THAN FACE-TO-FACE MEETINGS AND DISCUSS HOW YOU WILL ALL WELCOME OUR COMPUTERIZED ROBOT OVERLORDS.

# 2

# IN THE RESTROOM

Without a doubt, the most awkward place for small talk is the restroom.

Unless you find yourself in the restroom with your supervisor who insists on discussing business, they are not places for substantive professional conversations. Work issues are unwelcome anywhere within eye or earshot of a toilet, and should be kept to workstations or common areas. Similarly, though restrooms offer the illusion of privacy, they are not necessarily conducive for office gossip as someone you don't see or hear may be listening.

Excepting situations in which you find yourself in need of some sort of assistance, it's best to keep bathroom small talk to a minimum. Nobody wants to chat while doing their business, especially with someone standing or sitting right next to them (whether separated by a partition or not). Keep your small talk to the times before and after the main purpose of your trip, such as when you're entering, washing your hands, or exiting.

# Talking IRL IDEAS

**ANY TIME OF DAY:**
- I DO/DON'T LIKE THE KIND OF SOAP THEY HAVE IN THE DISPENSER.
- THIS WATER IS ALWAYS TOO HOT/COLD.

**IF IN THE MORNING:**
- GOOD MORNING. READY FOR THE DAY?

**IF IN THE AFTERNOON:**
- HI. HOW WAS LUNCH?

**IF AT THE END OF THE DAY:**
- WHAT A DAY, HUH? HAVE A GOOD NIGHT.

# ENCOUNTERING THE SAME PEOPLE
## IN THE RESTROOM

In one of the universe's crueler twists, you will inevitably find yourself encountering the same one or two people every time you have to use the facilities.

Make no mistake: it's a weird thing to experience, especially at first. The easiest and most obvious thing to do is acknowledge the ridiculousness of a shared timetable and say something along the lines of, "I guess we're on the same schedule!" or "I see you received the same eVite."

You'll both (or all) politely laugh at the absurdity of life and then retreat to your own stalls, trying to relieve yourselves while reconciling yourselves to the fact that your biological imperatives are somehow cosmically synchronized with someone who shares your email server and and 401K provider.

Sorry, but this is your life now.

But, after a few weeks or months, you'll both get used to it and probably forgo any small talk by simply nodding at one another before going about your business.

> > > > > > > > > > > > > > > > > > > > > > > > > > > > > > > >

# FYI

## > HANDWASHING <

*You must wash your hands before leaving the office restroom, even if you don't feel it's necessary (it is) and if you don't do so in the privacy of your own home (you should).*

*Because if another person in the restroom sees you not washing your hands, your not washing your hands will undoubtedly become the topic of small talk between that person and your other coworkers and you'll be known as the "person who doesn't wash their hands after using the restroom."*

## > ENCOUNTERING SUPERIORS <

*If you find yourself in the restroom with your superior, say hello or otherwise greet him or her, but do not try to engage your superior in conversation, as anything more substantive might go in an even more awkward direction: a discussion about business matters. Which would make your superior feel even more awkward, which will be remembered when he or she conducts your annual review.*

*If you find yourself on the same schedule with your superior, then you need to immediately change your schedule.*

# 3

# IDEAS FOR (ALMOST) ANY OCCASION

Unlike religion and politics (see pages 58-59), there are some topics of conversation that can be brought out in pretty much any situation. Because the answers are as ever changing as they are constant, they're as perfect to use with people you only meet once as they are with people you'll run into over and again.

# Talking IRL IDEAS

## THE WEATHER

You really can't go wrong with keeping a conversation about the weather. Weather is a demonstrable fact that everyone can experience in real time together, and we all have an opinion about it.

- IT'S SO BEAUTIFUL/HOT/COLD. IT JUST SEEMS SO BEAUTIFUL/HOT/COLD FOR THIS TIME OF YEAR.
- > TRY FOLLOWING UP BY MENTIONING THE DRASTIC **WEATHER CHANGE** FROM THE DAY BEFORE OR LAST YEAR AT THIS TIME, OR HOW MANY DAYS IT'S BEEN SO **BEAUTIFUL** OR TOO **COLD/HOT**.
- DO YOU KNOW THE FORECAST FOR TOMORROW/ NEXT WEEK?
- > NOW **YOU** EXPRESS PLEASURE/SURPRISE/ DISPLEASURE ABOUT THE FORECAST.

# MORE Talking IRL IDEAS

## SPORTS

Many people enjoy talking about sports, especially their local or favorite teams. Some people can literally talk for hours about it, so if you don't know as much about a team or sport, especially in a town or city that's not your own, just keep asking questions and they'll lead the conversation. You'll find this line will feel all the more natural if you're in a bar, restaurant, airport, or other place showing sporting events on televisions.

- HOW'S THE [LOCAL TEAM] DOING THIS YEAR?
- WHAT ARE THE TEAM'S PROSPECTS FOR THE CHAMPIONSHIP?
- HOW IS THE TEAM DOING COMPARED TO YEARS PAST?
- WHO ARE THE STAR PLAYERS AND HOW ARE THEY DOING?

- WHAT OTHER SPORTS ARE THEY INTO?
- DO THEY PLAY ANY SPORTS THEMSELVES?
> FOR ANY OF THESE QUESTIONS, TRY FOLLOWING UP WITH WHAT SPORTS **YOU** LIKE, WATCH, OR ARE INVOLVED IN.

# MOVIES, TELEVISION, MUSIC, THEATER, AND BOOKS

Movies, television, music, theater, and books offer people a common language to trade on, just like sports, with two notable exceptions: First, though you will certainly come across someone who claims that they're not into sports (and those who aren't into sports except for the Olympics), the chances of encountering someone who proclaims that they don't like books, movies, television, or music are insignificant. But should you happen upon one of these people, you must ask how they spend their time and then alert the authorities.

>>>>>>>>>>>>>>>>>>>>>>>>>>>>>>>>>>>>>>>>>>>

# MORE Talking IRL IDEAS

Second, though people likely root for teams based in or near their hometowns, there's no telling what media they enjoy, so you're likely to be presented with a veritable smorgasbord of titles, songs, and series to choose from.

## WHETHER YOU MEET A PERSON FOR THE FIRST TIME OR SEEM TO BUMP INTO SOMEONE EVERY TIME YOU STEP OUT ON AN ERRAND, TRY:

- WHAT MOVIES, TV SHOWS, OR BOOKS ARE YOU WATCHING OR READING NOW?
  > IF YOU'VE SEEN/READ THEM, SHARE YOUR THOUGHTS ON THEIR MERITS OR SHORTCOMINGS.
  > IF YOU'VE NOT SEEN/READ THEM, DESCRIBE YOUR

PLANS TO DO SO (OR VERY POLITELY SAY YOU'RE NOT USUALLY INTERESTED IN THAT PARTICULAR GENRE OR SUBJECT MATTER BUT WILL CERTAINLY CHECK IT OUT).

- WHAT MUSICIANS OR SINGERS DO YOU LIKE?
- DO THEY HAVE PARTICULAR ALBUMS OR SONGS THAT STAND OUT?

> NOW TALK ABOUT **YOUR** FAVORITE RECORDING ARTISTS OR PERFORMANCES.

- DO YOU GO TO THE THEATER FOR PLAYS/ MUSICALS/DANCE/OPERA?
- DO YOU ESPECIALLY LIKE ANY ENSEMBLES/ REPERTORY COMPANIES/DANCE TROUPES OR CONCERT HALLS/THEATERS? WHY DO YOU LIKE THEM?

> NOW TALK ABOUT **YOUR** FAVORITE VENUES FOR LIVE PERFORMANCES.

# MORE Talking IRL IDEAS

IF YOU'RE STUCK NEXT TO SOMEONE AND CAN'T ACTUALLY READ YOUR BOOK, WATCH YOUR MOVIE OR EPISODE, OR LISTEN TO YOUR MUSIC, ASK:

- WHAT UPCOMING MOVIES, SHOWS, OR BOOKS ARE YOU LOOKING FORWARD TO?
- > NOW SHARE WHAT **YOU** EXPECT TO BE WATCHING OR READING IN THE NEAR FUTURE.
- WHAT MOVIES, SHOWS, OR BOOKS CURRENTLY OUT HAVEN'T YOU SEEN/READ YET?
- > NOW SHARE **YOUR** TO-WATCH/READ LIST.

## ASK HOW THEY WATCH ENTIRE SERIES THAT ARE DROPPED AS A WHOLE ON STREAMING SERVICES.

• DO YOU BINGE ALL EPISODES AT ONCE? OR WATCH THEM BIT BY BIT TO PROLONG THE EXPERIENCE?

> NOW SHARE HOW **YOU** WATCH THEM.

• HOW MANY EPISODES HAVE YOU WATCHED IN A ROW?

> NOW SHARE **YOUR** TOP NUMBER.

• HOW MUCH OF A CHANCE DO YOU GIVE SHOWS TO CAPTURE YOUR ATTENTION? ONE EPISODE? TWO?

• DO YOU HAVE TO FINISH WATCHING WHATEVER YOU STARTED?

> NOW TALK ABOUT HOW QUICKLY **YOU** FORM OPINIONS AND WHETHER OR NOT **YOU** PUSH YOURSELF TO COMPLETE A SERIES.

# MORE Talking IRL IDEAS

## VACATIONS AND WEEKENDS

Everyone looks forward to not having to be at work or school. Even if the person you're speaking with is retired, unemployed, or underemployed, everyone treasures time away from work.

## IF YOU NEED TO MAKE SMALL TALK DURING THE WEEK OR BEFORE A HOLIDAY, ASK:

- WHAT ARE YOUR PLANS FOR THE UPCOMING WEEKEND, LONG WEEKEND, OR HOLIDAY BREAK?
- > NOW DESCRIBE WHAT **YOUR** PLANS ARE.

## IF IT'S A MONDAY OR A DAY JUST AFTER A HOLIDAY, ASK:

- WHAT DID YOU DO THIS PAST WEEKEND/HOLIDAY BREAK?

> NOW TALK ABOUT WHAT **YOU** DID.

# FYI

## > GET OUTTA HERE <

*It's always appropriate to ask about people's vacation plans, especially at the beginning of the summer. And you can never go wrong asking if someone has any trips or vacations planned for the upcoming months.*

*And it's totally okay to follow up by talking about your plans.*

> > > > > > > > > > > > > > > > > > > > > > > > > > > > > > > > > > > > ●

# DEATH AND OTHER AWKWARD SITUATIONS

Sometimes bad things happen to good people, and sometimes, bad things happen to bad people, which is nice in its own way. But that's for another book.

As you live your life, you're going to find yourself in more and more awkward situations. People are going to die. They are going to break up or get divorced. They are going to lose their jobs. Their team is going to lose the championship, which doesn't really count as a bad thing for them personally, but we all sort of get why people get upset by that.

# Contents

# FUNERALS

Funerals are the worst. Especially if it's yours. But, chances are, you'll only attend one of your own funeral while you'll have to go to lots of other peoples' as you age. The good thing about funerals is that usually nobody's in a particularly chatty mood, so the need for small talk decreases exponentially.

> > > > > > > > > > > > > > > > > > > > > > > > > > > > > > > > > > >

# Talking IRL IDEAS

FIRST TELL THE BEREAVED HOW SORRY YOU ARE FOR THEIR LOSS. IF YOU DO NOT KNOW THE BEREAVED, YOU COULD SAY:

- I WOULD HAVE LIKED TO HAVE MET YOU UNDER BETTER CIRCUMSTANCES.

> YOU COULD FOLLOW UP BY **ASKING TO BE INTRODUCED** TO THE BEREAVED'S LOVED ONES AND EXTEND YOUR SYMPATHIES TO THEM.

> THIS IS NOT NECESSARILY THE TIME TO SHARE YOUR **PERSONAL STORIES** OF LOSS, BUT IF THEY ASK, FOCUS ON THE GOOD THINGS YOU REMEMBER ABOUT THE LOVED ONE.

> IF THEY'RE WILLING, FOLLOW UP BY ASKING THEM TO SHARE A **HAPPY MEMORY**.

# FYI

## THIS PARTICULAR SITUATION
## > ISN'T, FOR ONCE, ABOUT YOU, <
## SO THINK OF OTHERS

*Most family and friends of the deceased are physically and emotionally exhausted, and, when faced with an acquaintance, will want to keep the conversation as fleeting as possible.*

*They may turn conversation to the more mundane aspects of the event, including how you got to the funeral home or cemetery, or topics that let them live vicariously through you, like what your plans are for after the funeral.*

*Answer their questions, but don't gloat. It's okay to say you have plans with some friends, but it's not okay to say you're all so excited to get the hell out of there and run to the opening night of a movie everyone on earth has been waiting eleven years for and isn't a bummer that they're stuck mourning while you'll be stuffing your face with popcorn?*

>>>>>>>>>>>>>>>>>>>>>>>>>>>>>>>>>>>>>>>>>>

# BTW

## > LOOK ON THE BRIGHT SIDE <

*Chances are you're going to know at least one other person at any given funeral. Of course, you could know many people, for example, if your Saturday football league's teammate's grandfather passes away peacefully at age one hundred: in that case, you'll know your teammate and the rest of the team so you'll just need to express your sympathies and then rejoin the huddle in the corner.*

*But even if you only know one other person, such as the bereaved, the majority of funerals and burials are occupied by respectful and solemn silent contemplation, so you're really in a good spot, conversationally speaking.*

# 2

# BREAKUPS **AND** DIVORCES

You may be familiar with the term *schadenfreude*, which means taking pleasure in other people's failure or suffering. Though not technically one of the Seven Deadly Sins, it's not a nice thing to do. But, c'mon, between us, it is sometimes a little satisfying when that shady lady named Karma provides comeuppance to the ne'er-do-wells who cross your path (even though she may take a while).

Just keep your joy to yourself or—if you must—to your closest and dearest who may sympathize and join with you in toasting the breakup of a rival's marriage. And though you might have ample justification for celebrating a friend or frenemy being left at the altar, there's no rational excuse to feel that way about someone you barely know.

# FYI

## > WHAT GOES AROUND <

*Even if it's your dreaded coworker who cries while signing off on your requisition forms, an unhelpful airline employee who can't get you on the next flight to Des Moines because the hurricane blowing outside rivals that of the one in his broken heart, or the accountant auditing your taxes whose desk is littered with face-down photo frames—you really can't, or at least shouldn't, be made happy by their misery. The only thing you can do is indulge them with a little small talk to help ease their minds.*

*Do remember, though, that there's a fine line between small talk and prying, so it's best to let the other person lead the tone of the conversation.*

>>>>>>>>>>>>>>>>>>>>>>>>>>>>>>>>>>>>>>

# Talking IRL IDEAS

## ONCE SOMEONE TELLS YOU THEY'VE HAD A BREAKUP OR DIVORCE, GENTLY ASK:

• HOW ARE YOU DEALING WITH IT?

> FOLLOW UP BY OFFERING TO **HELP** IN ANY WAY YOU CAN, WHETHER IT'S PICKING UP THE KIDS FROM SCHOOL OR PICKING UP THE SLACK AT THE OFFICE.

## BTW

However juicy your own breakup or divorce story, or however wronged you may still feel about your own situation, do not offer stories about your own breakup. Nobody in the throes of a relationship breakdown wants to hear about anyone else's.

SOMETIMES IT'S OKAY JUST TO LISTEN. WHEN YOU DO SPEAK, KEEP TO SHORT, DECLARATIVE STATEMENTS LIKE:

- WHAT A TOUGH SITUATION.
- SOUNDS LIKE YOU'RE GOING THROUGH A ROUGH TIME.
- TAKES A LOT OF COURAGE TO DO WHAT'S BEST FOR YOU.
- NO, GOING ON A HONEYMOON ALONE ISN'T HUMILIATING AT ALL.

IF THERE ARE KIDS OR PETS, ASK:

- HOW ARE THEY DOING OR ADJUSTING TO THE CHANGE?

# FYI

### > ABOUT CUSTODY <

*Do not ask about custody, or who the kids or pets like better.*

### > ABOUT DATES <

*Do not use the opportunity to ask the person out on a date, or set them up with your cousin who, truth be told, would be perfect for someone on the rebound.*

### > ABOUT THE EX <

*If you know the ex, make sure to keep your opinion about that person to yourself. You never know if they're going to get back together, and you don't want to set yourself up for even more awkward conversations.*

# BTW

*Do not be fooled, when undergoing a dental procedure, into thinking that you're immune from small talk. Dental professionals love trying to make you chat with a mouth full of gauze. Do not try to talk or you'll choke on your own spit or frustration.*

*Instead, practice making noises that sound like "Yes," "No," and "Listen, I get that you're trying to be friendly, but that drill is super close to a nerve and I'd like to just sit here quietly for a few moments and, by the way, do you validate parking?"*

# GRACEFUL EXITS

Some people say that it's the journey, not the destination that matters. These are people who have never had to win a swim meet, fly home for Thanksgiving, or find a bathroom RIGHT NOW I MEAN IT OH NO THERE'S SOMEONE IN THERE WHAT ARE THEY DOING WHY ARE THEY TAKING SO LONG OH NO.

Similarly, I bet you'll agree that when embarking on a journey of small talk, the only thing that matters is the destination, which is "away from this journey."

Though you should never just stop talking and stare at the person until they feel so uncomfortable that they walk away, there are some easy—and kind—ways to get yourself out of a situation.

# Talking IRL IDEAS

> PRETEND TO SEE SOMEONE YOU MUST TALK TO.
> CHECK YOUR WATCH AND "REMEMBER" AN APPOINTMENT.
> PRETEND YOUR PHONE HAS BUZZED SILENTLY AND YOU "NEED TO TAKE AN IMPORTANT CALL."*
> KINDLY AND GENTLY EXPLAIN THAT IT'S BEEN A PLEASURE CHATTING, BUT YOU'RE INVESTED IN WHATEVER IT WAS YOU WERE DOING.
> ADMIT THAT YOU'RE FINDING THEIR THOUGHTS ON INDONESIAN MICROLOANS FASCINATING, BUT YOU ASSUME THEY'D PREFER QUIET WHILE THEY PERFORM YOUR PROCTOLOGIC EXAMINATION.

*This only works if your phone is with you and the other person cannot see your blank screen.

# A **FINID IMPORTANT** NOTE

There are approximately 7.7 billion people on the Earth. By my last estimate, approximately 7.65 billion of them are as uncertain about talking to someone IRL as you are. So don't worry too much about not knowing exactly what to say all the time; chances are the other person is searching for what to say as much as you are and, together, you will be able to navigate the silence between you.

On a personal note, based on the above population estimate, we printed about 7.65 billion copies of this book so it would be super great if you could recommend this book to them.

>>>>>>>>>>>>>>>>>>>>>>>>>>>>>>>>>>>>>>>>>

# ACKNOWLEDGMENTS

Talking IRL with my editor Elizabeth Smith, designer Celina Carvalho, production manager Barbara Sadick, and publicist Antonia Paruolo not only passes the time in the happiest of ways, but makes me a better writer and person. Don't know what it does to them, though. I must give special acknowledgment to my puppy, Oscar, who has forced me to make small talk with his dog friends, their owners, and pet-shop personnel during our daily outings.

First published in the United States of America in 2020 by
Universe Publishing, A Division of
Rizzoli International Publications, Inc.
300 Park Avenue South
New York, NY 10010
www.rizzoliusa.com

Copyright © 2020 Robb Pearlman

Publisher: Charles Miers
Editor: Elizabeth Smith
Design: Celina Carvalho
Production Manager: Barbara Sadick
Managing Editor: Lynn Scrabis

Printed in China

2020 2021 2022 2023 / 10 9 8 7 6 5 4 3 2 1

ISBN: 978-0-7893-3701-6
Library of Congress Control Number: 2019947963

Visit us online:
Facebook.com/RizzoliNewYork
Twitter: @Rizzoli_Books
Instagram.com/RizzoliBooks
Pinterest.com/RizzoliBooks
Youtube.com/user/RizzoliNY
Issuu.com/Rizzoli

I believe in

_____

I don't know
what to say!

I want to be a _____
WHEN I GROW UP.

I'D RATHER _____
THAN _____.

I'M GOING TO

_____

WHEN THIS IS OVER.

I'M GOING TO

_____

WHEN THIS IS OVER.

I'M A

_____

I'M A

_____

I'M JUST HERE
FOR THE _____.

I'M JUST HERE
FOR THE _____.

I just binge-watched

_____

I just binge-watched

_____

DON'T ASK ME ABOUT

MY FAVORITE MOVIE IS _____.

I STAN
_____.

Ask me about my
_____.

I'M FROM

I'M FROM

I like stickers, do you?

I like stickers, do you?